Meet Martin Luther

by
Pamela Honan Peterson

_____
my name

_____
date

Exploring Luther's Small Catechism

Augsburg Fortress
Minneapolis

Contents

1. From Fear to Faith .. 2
2. God Gives Us Courage 8
3. Helping People Know God's Love 13
4. Luther and the New Church 19

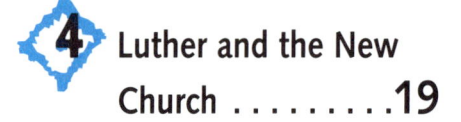

**Meet Martin Luther
Exploring Luther's Small Catechism
Learner Resource**

This Learner Resource has a corresponding Leader Leaflet.

Pamela Honan Peterson, writer
Mary Nasby Lohre and Alyn Beckman, editors
Jack Kershner, illustrator
RKB Studios, Inc., designer
Jim Whitmer, cover photograph

Scripture acknowledgement: Scripture quotations marked NRSV are from New Revised Standard Version Bible, copyright 1989 Division of Christian Education of the National Council of the Churches of Christ in the United States of America. Used by permission.

Excerpts are reprinted from Martin Luther: Giant of Faith, copyright © 1981 Augsburg Publishing House and The Story of Luther's Small Catechism, copyright © 1982 Augsburg Publishing House.

Copyright © 1995 Augsburg Fortress
All rights reserved. May not be reproduced.

ISBN 0-8066-6784-2

Printed on 50% recycled paper, minimum 10% postconsumer content.

Manufactured in U.S.A.
1 2 3 4 5 6 7 8 9 0 1 2 3 4 5 6 7 8 9

1 From Fear to Faith

Changes and Fears

Martin Luther was born in Germany in 1483. He grew up to be a courageous leader and reformer in the Christian church. (A *reformer* is someone who works to improve or change something that is wrong or is not working well.) But some strange, scary, and wonderful things happened to him first.

Martin was born in an exciting time of change. He was your age when Christopher Columbus landed in America. Other adventurers were exploring China at the same time. The printing press had been invented, so books could be printed in large numbers. Many people could learn about the world from them.

However, most people in Luther's day had very little education. Their hearts and minds were full of fears and superstitions. They believed God would punish them for every mistake they made. Martin was afraid of God, too.

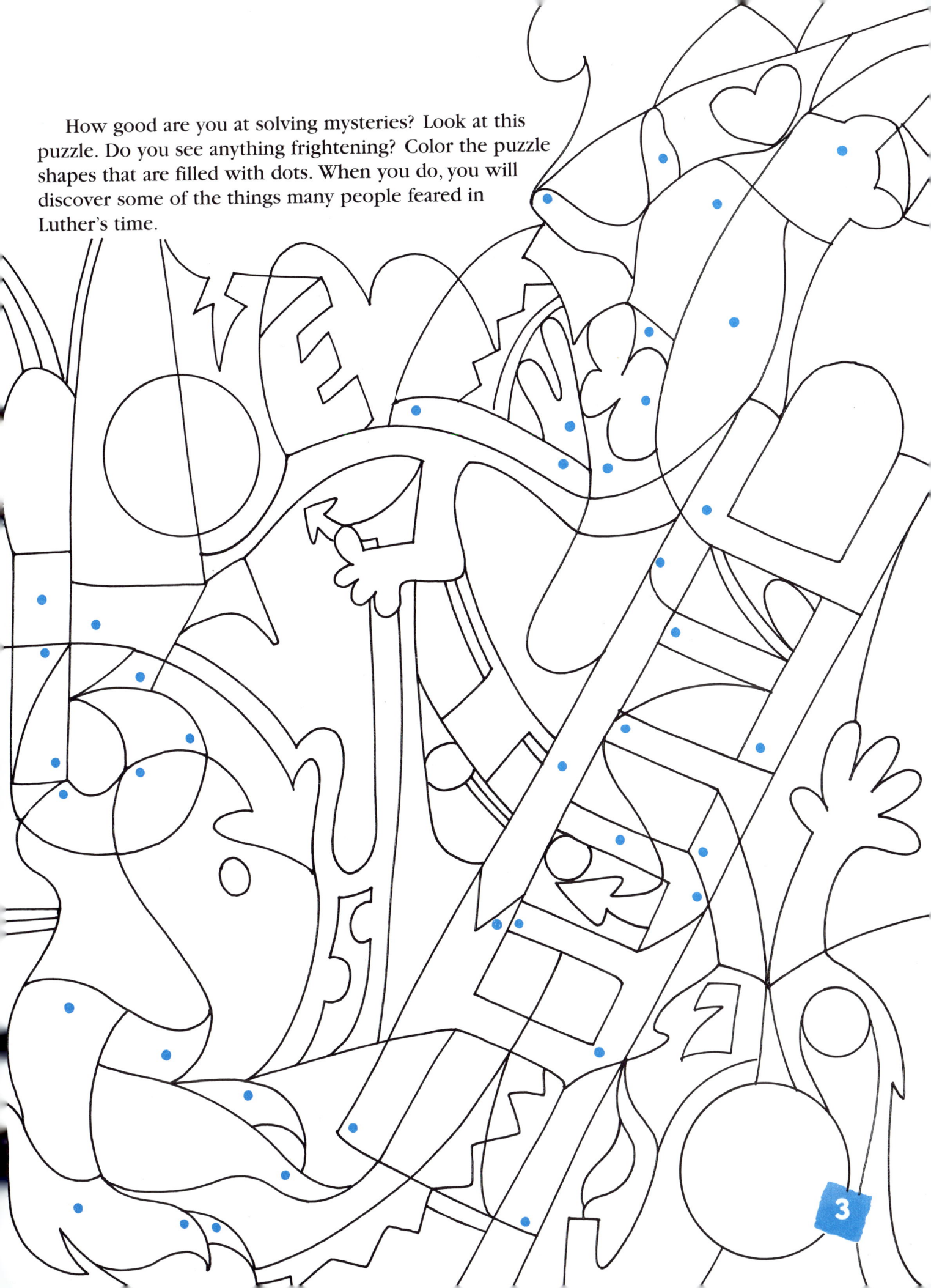

How good are you at solving mysteries? Look at this puzzle. Do you see anything frightening? Color the puzzle shapes that are filled with dots. When you do, you will discover some of the things many people feared in Luther's time.

A Storm and a Search

One day when Martin was a grown man, lightning struck a tree near where he was standing. Martin believed God was threatening to punish him for his sins. He was very afraid! In fact, he promised to become a monk if God saved him from the storm.

As a monk, Martin studied the Bible many hours a day. He searched for words that would make him sure God would forgive his sins and take him to heaven when he died. He studied the Bible continuously as he worked as a pastor and professor, trying to please God and earn God's forgiveness. But he never felt like he was pleasing God enough. And he never felt forgiven.

Look for the Words

What words from the Bible help us know how much God loves us and forgives us? Some of those words are listed next to the puzzle. Circle each word when you find it.

WORD LIST
- ANGER
- FAITH
- FEAR
- HOPE
- I FORGIVE YOU
- JESUS CARES
- JOY
- LOVE
- PEACE
- PUNISH

```
H O P E F E E P L T W G
I F O R G I V E Y O U E
J X P N O R B A B L T L
E N V X C P O C D W R R
S H F A I T H E W J N E
U X J M M E V L T R H C
S T V W P U N I S H A L
C K Y F D O O U Y X T O
A N G E R A N Z H A C V
R I W A T H E D L J W E
E T Z R E A L T B O R B
S C F D A N Y L E Y M K
```

Martin Tries to Make Changes

Martin kept reading the Bible, trying to find answers to his questions and fears about God. One day a preacher named Johann Tetzel came to Wittenburg, the town where Luther lived. He said that if people bought slips of paper he was selling for the leaders of the church, they could get to heaven more easily. Choose parts and do this skit to see what happened.

GIRL: Look at the bonfire! What's going on?

BOY: I don't know. Listen. There's music—and look at all the people. Let's go see what it is.

TETZEL: Come one, come all! Look at this big, hot fire. This is how God will punish people for their sins!

ALL: Oooh!

TETZEL: But you can be safe from this kind of punishment. Buy these little papers from the head of the church. Many of your sins will be forgiven with each paper you buy. You won't have to fear the fires of hell after all.

CHURCH MEMBER 1: I'll buy them!

CHURCH MEMBER 2: So will I. This is good news!

LUTHER, to Tetzel: Why are you selling these indulgences? It is wrong.

TETZEL: We need money to build a great church in Rome. When we sell these, we make money and the people are happy. What does it hurt?

LUTHER, to church members: Why don't you come to church anymore?

CHURCH MEMBER 1: We bought indulgences. We have "paid for" our sins. We don't need to go to church now.

LUTHER: That is wrong. The Bible does not say we can buy God's forgiveness. It says we must be sorry for our sins. And only God can forgive our sins, not another person—not even the head of the church!

(A few days later.)

LUTHER: Where's my hammer? I'm going to nail this list of 95 reasons to the church door. Then people will know why indulgences and some other things church leaders are doing are wrong. If I nail these here on the door, other professors may read them and we can discuss them. Maybe we can get the church leaders to change their ways.

PROFESSOR: Look at this list! I agree with Luther. Many of these things are wrong.

PRINTER: Let me see it. Hm-m-m. I agree too. I am going to make copies of all 95 statements on my printing press so everyone can read them. These things should be changed. I wonder what the church leaders in Rome will do if they see this list.

POPE LEO X, in Rome: Look at this list someone sent me! Martin Luther is daring to say that many things in the church need to change. Who does he think he is? I will order him to stop!

Everything Changed

Martin went on teaching and talking about things that needed to be changed in the church. But he never forgot his fears about God being an angry, punishing God. He kept searching the Bible for answers to his fears.

Then everything changed one night. Martin was reading the Bible when he saw the truth at last. "We don't have to earn God's forgiveness," he thought. "Jesus did that for us. We only accept God's forgiveness as a gift by faith!"

When Martin discovered this amazing treasure of God's truth, his fears vanished. The sun shone in his heart.

This is one of the Bible verses that helped Martin learn the truth about God. Read it together and put it in your own words in the coin on the right. Then write a sentence prayer below thanking God for forgiving you freely through Jesus. Take turns praying your prayers.

For by grace you have been saved through faith, and this is not your own doing; it is the gift of God.
Ephesians 2:8 NRSV

God Gives Us Courage

It Takes Courage

Sometimes it takes courage to do what we know is right. Find a partner or a small group to join. Read together about each of the following situations. Role-play the way you would respond. Then talk about whether or not your response would take courage. What belief would you be standing up for in each situation?

1. You are late getting home from school because you and your friend hung out at the video store—even though your parent asked you not to do that. If you tell the truth about where you were, you'll be grounded. Your friend says, "Don't tell!"

2. The new kid in town seems shy and lonely. While you're waiting in the lunch line by him, you want to invite him to sit with you. But you know if you do, the popular kids will give you a bad time.

3. You saw two kids in the bushes during the lunch hour drinking from a can of beer. They know you saw them. If they get in trouble, they'll be sure you reported them.

4. Some kids tease Simon about his religious beliefs—especially the little cap he wears all the time. They decide to gang up and grab it from him after school. They ask you to join them.

Luther Needed Courage Too

Some church leaders were angry with Martin Luther for saying that some things needed to be changed. One church leader challenged Luther to a debate so they could talk about their disagreements. But at that debate, he asked Luther questions that tricked him into saying things that got him into trouble with the head of the church. The pope was so unhappy with Luther's answers that he told Luther he could no longer be a member of the church.

Luther was sad. He did not want to leave the church. He just wanted to help make it better. But he knew he must stand up for what he believed the Bible taught. He also knew that some people wanted to kill him for what he was saying. But he kept on talking about his beliefs.

What do you think helped Luther have the courage to say what he believed? Unscramble the word in each box to find out where Luther got his courage. Can these things also help YOU have the courage to do what is right?

1. _____

2. _____

3. _____

4. _____

On Trial!

Because of his writings, Luther was ordered to go on trial before the emperor. His friends feared for his life. But Luther sang hymns all the way to the trial!

At the trial, Luther was told to take back all he had written and said about the church. He refused because he knew he could not turn his back on his discovery that eternal life is a free gift from God through faith. "I cannot," he said. "Here I stand. God help me."

The emperor then declared him to be an outlaw. (That meant anyone could kill him without fearing punishment.) Use the code to discover the Bible verses that may have given Luther courage during this time. Later, Luther wrote his most famous hymn about these verses.

Code:

A = ✓　　N = ∪
B = △　　O = □
C = †　　P = ∨
D = ~　　Q = ↑
E = ≺　　R = ⋋
F = ⋋　　S = ∇
G = ⌈　　T = ✕
H = ✻　　U = ⋏
I = ⊊　　V = ⊥
J = 3　　W = ε
K = −　　X = ⋅†⋅
L = ∧　　Y = ∪
M = ⌒　　Z = ϕ

___ ___ ___ is our ___ ___ ___ ___ ___ ___ ___ and strength, a ___ ___ ___ ___ present ___ ___ ___ ___ in trouble. Therefore, we ___ ___ ___ ___ ___ ___ ___ ___ .... The ___ ___ ___ ___ of hosts is ___ ___ ___ ___ ___ ___ .

Psalm 46:1-2,7 NRSV

Let's Pray

Because we are Jesus' followers, it is important for us to believe what the Bible teaches us and to stand up for those beliefs. Like Luther, we can depend on Jesus to help us. We can also depend on each other.

For prayer time, we will make a prayer web to remind us that we are all connected together by God's love. We can help each other obey and serve God.

What would you like God to help you do? How can you encourage someone else? Write about it here.

God, help me encourage others to:

Flashlight Fun

The word *courage* comes from the Latin word for heart. When English-speaking people want to encourage someone, they sometimes say, "Take heart."

Have some fun making a "Take Heart" poster to remind yourself to have courage. Your teacher will have the materials you need. Find a partner and have some flashlight fun!

Directions

1. Print "TAKE HEART" at the top of a piece of drawing paper.

2. Cut a heart shape out of stiff paper.

3. Notice the slit on the top of the drinking straw. Put the heart shape in the slit to hold it in place.

4. Hold the heart shape over the drawing paper. Shine a flashlight on the shape to make a shadow. Try holding the light or the shape at different angles, so the shadow changes. It will not always look exactly like a heart.

5. Trace the shapes you see on different parts of the paper. Trace it a couple of times when it looks like a heart. Other times it can look more like something else. Fill the paper with designs.

6. Color the shapes. You may want to use both crayons and markers to get softer and brighter effects.

Helping People Know God's Love 3

Kidnapped!

After the trial at Worms, Martin Luther began his trip home to Wittenberg. He knew the emperor had labeled him an outlaw. That meant anyone could capture and kill him without punishment. He hoped he would get home safely. Suddenly, a group of armed men jumped out of the forest! They tied Luther up and carried him off to an old castle.

But these kidnappers were not out to harm Luther! Instead, they were Luther's friends who had kidnapped him to hide him from the emperor. They hid him in the Wartburg Castle disguised as a knight.

God protected Luther from being killed by sending friends to hide him. God also protects and cares for all of us in many ways. Some of those ways are surprising. In each castle window, draw or write about one way in which God protects you from danger or helps you during scary or difficult times. Be ready to explain what you have done.

13

The Bible

The Wartburg Castle was a lonely and quiet place. But Luther put his time alone there to good use. He translated the New Testament into simple German, the language spoken by most of the people of his country. Why do you think he did that?

Well, Luther believed that the Bible is the only book that tells people what is true about God. He taught that everything else we read about God must agree with what the Bible says or it is not true. Luther believed that people should be able to read the Bible easily so they could understand these truths.

But most of the Bibles in Luther's time were written in Latin—an ancient language that most of the people did not understand. Luther knew that even those who could read this other language would benefit from studying the Bible in their own language. Luther wanted everyone to be able to read the Bible and learn from it about God and God's plans for their lives.

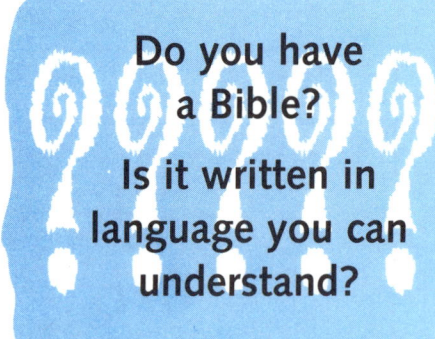

Do you have a Bible? Is it written in language you can understand?

Try It Out

What do you think it was like for the people in Luther's day to try to understand the Bible when they couldn't read the language in which it was written? Try this game. See how difficult it is to understand something when you don't know how to read it.

Directions

Follow the letters from right to left. There are no spaces between words, but there are periods at the end of sentences.

Read all of the directions; then do what they say to do.

Work in pairs. See which pair finishes first!

```
O H C A E O T I H Y A S
N O E D A R T . R E H T
C A E H T I W E O H S E
R A P O H . R E H T O H
O M O O R E H T D N U O
S P P U K O O L . E C N
W . 3 0 1 : 9 1 1 M L A
    : E R E H T I E T I R
```

_____
_____
_____
_____

Which was easier—reading the directions on this page or reading the Psalm verse? Why was that true?

What do you think this Psalm verse means? Why are God's words compared with sweet honey?

Share God's Love with a Song

After a year at Wartburg Castle, it was safe for Luther to return home to Wittenberg. There he could return to his teaching, writing, and preaching. He wanted to find many ways to help people discover the true message of God's love that is found in the Bible.

Luther loved to sing and play music. So he wrote many hymns to help explain the Bible in simple words and melodies that people could understand and enjoy.

Here is a simple hymn about God's love. Sing it to the tune of "Twinkle, Twinkle, Little Star." Finish the verses you see. Then try to write a whole verse of your own.

1. God loves you, and God loves me.
   We are all God's family.
   Our friend Jesus from above
   Comes to us to share God's love.
   _____
   _____

2. Jesus, Jesus is our friend,
   Gives us life that never ends.
   "Thank you, Jesus," we all sing.
   "We love you, our awesome king!"
   _____
   _____

3. _____
   _____
   _____
   _____
   _____

A Very Special Book

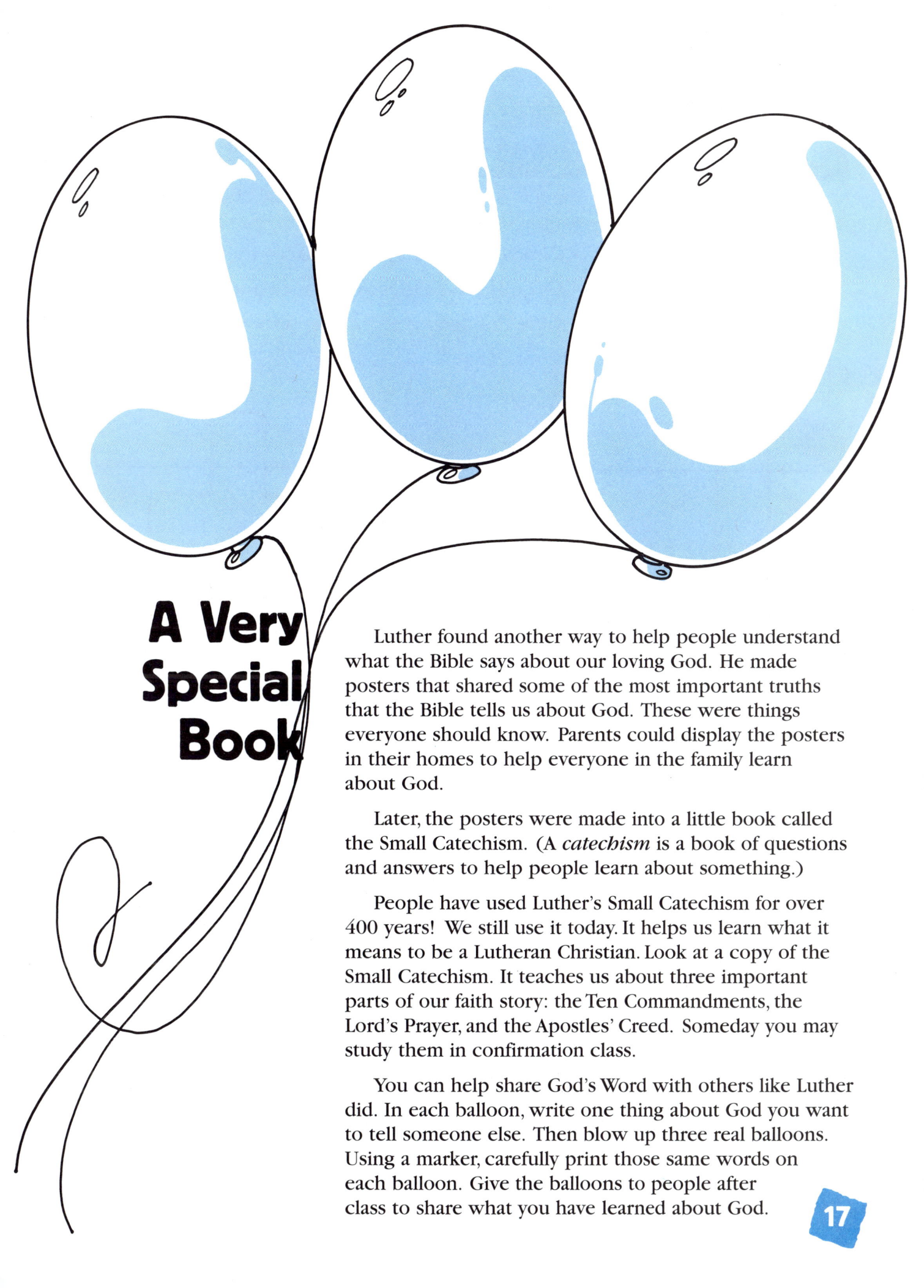

Luther found another way to help people understand what the Bible says about our loving God. He made posters that shared some of the most important truths that the Bible tells us about God. These were things everyone should know. Parents could display the posters in their homes to help everyone in the family learn about God.

Later, the posters were made into a little book called the Small Catechism. (A *catechism* is a book of questions and answers to help people learn about something.)

People have used Luther's Small Catechism for over 400 years! We still use it today. It helps us learn what it means to be a Lutheran Christian. Look at a copy of the Small Catechism. It teaches us about three important parts of our faith story: the Ten Commandments, the Lord's Prayer, and the Apostles' Creed. Someday you may study them in confirmation class.

You can help share God's Word with others like Luther did. In each balloon, write one thing about God you want to tell someone else. Then blow up three real balloons. Using a marker, carefully print those same words on each balloon. Give the balloons to people after class to share what you have learned about God.

Make a Reminder

Make a book mark for your Bible to remind you to thank God for this special book. If you do not want to use your ribbon as a bookmark, you could display it in your room to remind you of God's special book for God's people. Follow these directions:

- **Choose three shapes and trace them.**
- **Cut out the shapes you traced and decorate them.**
- **Glue the decorated shapes on a ribbon.**

Luther and the New Church

Changes and a New Church

Martin Luther worked very hard for many years trying to help people learn about God. He wrote 100 books and some music. He translated the New Testament into German. He also got married. He and his wife Katie had six children. The whole family loved to sing while Luther played the lute for them.

Luther had begun his work wanting only to help the church make the Word of God the basis for its teaching. But when the church refused to change and made him leave, he and his followers began a new church. Luther called the church "Evangelical," which means "good news." Some people started to call this church "Lutheran." Luther did not want the church named after him, but the name stuck. The Lutheran church is still alive and well today in many countries.

Changes are not always easy. Put yourself in Luther's place in these times of change. Then fill in the blank spaces to answer these questions:

How do you think Luther felt in each situation?
Who could have helped Luther in difficult times?

1
Luther's feelings:

Luther's helpers:

2
Luther's feelings:

Luther's helpers:

3
Luther's feelings:

Luther's helpers:

4
Luther's feelings:

Luther's helpers:

Remember when a change happened in your life. Was it scary, happy, or sad? Who helped you?

Luther's Life

Can you remember some of the many important things that happened during Luther's lifetime? Here is a fun way to remember. Follow Luther's steps as you move from START to FINISH.

Game Directions

- Cut a coin-size paper circle for each player. Each player should write his or her initials on a paper circle.

- Two to four players may use one playing board.

- Cut 20 one-inch paper squares for players to use. Number them 1 through 4. Keep the squares upside down in a pile.

- Each player will, in turn, draw a number and move that number of spaces.

- Read aloud any "event" square on which you land.

- The player who finishes first wins!

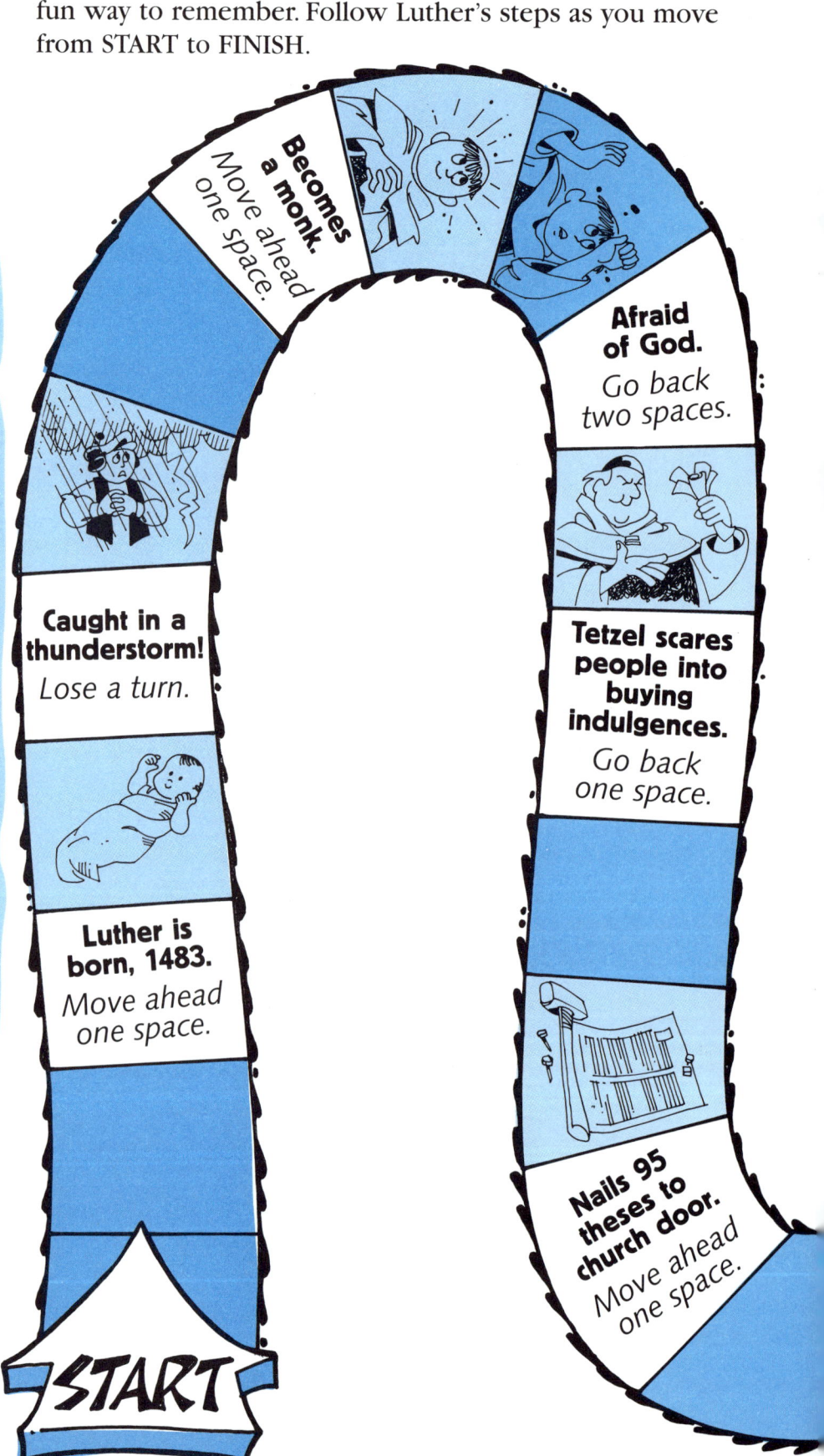

Board spaces (from START to FINISH):

- START
- Luther is born, 1483. Move ahead one space.
- Caught in a thunderstorm! Lose a turn.
- Becomes a monk. Move ahead one space.
- Afraid of God. Go back two spaces.
- Tetzel scares people into buying indulgences. Go back one space.
- Nails 95 theses to church door. Move ahead one space.

20

Goes on trial
Go back one space.

Church leaders make Luther leave the church.
Lose a turn.

Discovers God's love is a free gift.
Take an extra turn.

Hides out in Wartburg Castle.
Lose a turn.

Translates the New Testament into German.
Go ahead two spaces.

Returns home and resumes teaching.
Go ahead one space.

Gets married and has six children.
Go ahead one space.

Begins a new church centered on Bible teachings.
Go ahead one space.

FINISH

Luther's Church Today

Today, 500 years after Luther lived, the Lutheran church is active all over the world. "Martin Snooper," the great dog detective, sniffed out some interesting facts about this church. But by mistake, his damp nose erased some of the ink! Can you fill in the missing letters so we can get all the facts?

#1 There are about ___,___,___ Lutherans in the world.

#2 Biblical _____ is still the center of Lutheran faith.

#3 The Lutheran Church helps many people who face _____ and _____.

#4 The Lutheran Church sends _____ to tell people Jesus loves them and died for them.

#5 Both _____ and ___ can be pastors.

#6 The Lutheran church works to _____ Christians.

Ask your pastor to tell you more about the work of the Lutheran church today in your neighborhood and around the world.

22

Me and My Lutheran Church

What do you know about your Lutheran church? Fill in all the information you can. Then ask your pastor or another leader in your congregation to help you find the answers you need.

1. The name of my congregation is:

2. My congregation began in:

3. Two things I really like about my congregation are:

4. Some ways my congregation tells people the good news about Jesus' love are:

5. Some ways my congregation shows God's love by helping people are:

A Special Sign

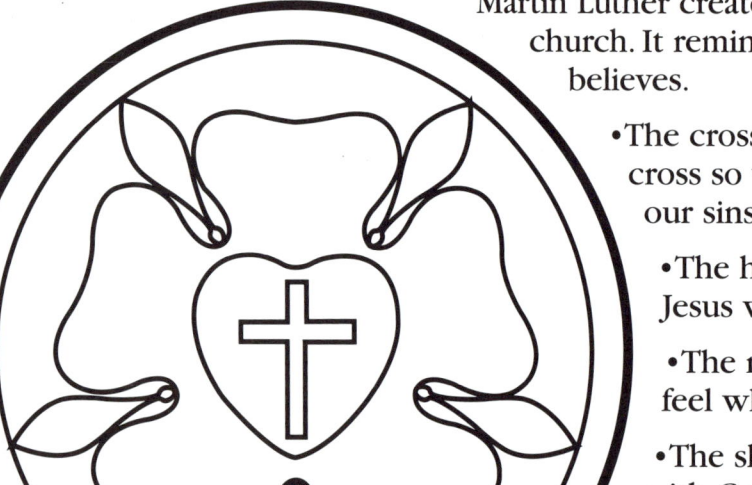

Martin Luther created a special seal for the new church. It reminds people what the new church believes.

- The cross reminds us that Jesus died on the cross so we can be forgiven by God for all our sins. Color it gold.
- The heart reminds us that we believe in Jesus with all our heart. Color it red.
- The rose reminds us of the peace we feel when we believe. Leave it white.
- The sky reminds us of the joy we share with God when we believe. Color it blue.
- The ring reminds us that this joy will never end. Color it gold.

Design two seals to show what is important to you about Jesus and your church. Choose one of your designs to decorate a medallion for you to keep to help you remember that Jesus guides you and your church in all that you do. Your leader will give you the art supplies you need.